JAPA:

THE UNTOLD STORY OF HUMAN MIGRATION (ACASEOF NIGERIA)

By

Ndubuisi Obi T.

Prepared and typeset at
Prime Edge Publishers.
(A Subsidiary of Prime Edge Ventures)
E-mail: primedgepublishers@yahoo.com
Tel: +2348063221583, +2347014218508
Federal Republic of Nigeria by
First Published
In KDP Amazon
ISBN:9-798-3231-7821 -6

All biblical quotations are from
THE HOLY BIBLE
NEW INTERNATIONAL VERSION

DEDICATION

I dedicate this work to my Spiritual son, Michael Chiemerie Agbasoga and other children of Nigerian parents who have joined the mass movement described as "JAPA" to seek better means of life explorations and discoveries in the absence of meaningful future for them in the nation, Nigeria.

APPRECIATION

Writing is like creation, bringing your thoughts and emotions into reality

This book was written under anger and helplessness. As I watch our able bodied men, women and children migrate out of the nation in the ferocious SPIRIT of JAPA, I get angry at seeing the workforce of this nation disappear into the prepared ground of the developed nations; helpless because there is nothing I could do to halt the mass exodus.

Without great friends and acquaintances around me, I could not have succeeded in this journey to highlight the causes and solutions to this daily migration of citizens in search of a better climate for existence.

My candid thanks goes to Chief Dr. Michael Ikuku, who has been giving me and my family rice seasonally for the past five seasons just as he extends to numerous people, known or unknown to him

To Mrs. Justina Uzowulu who has been in remembrance of her husband's brother, especially at critical periods of my life when hope seemed lost.

To Collins Aghaegbulem Eghomien whose financial help during the burial of my sister helped to open the floodgate of financial support for me at this challenging time.

To Anosike Greg who showed great interest in my wellbeing morally and financially even when he too is passing through challenges that could dwarf many.

To Ofili Nwokedi for the years of friendship! A friend indeed!

To my own Reverend father, John Paul Uzochukwu whose pragmatic approach to my many periods of Valley experiences has been uplifting.

To Casmir Chiekezie whose support over the years gives credence to the value of true friendship!

And to my family members for condoning my near recluse life during the preparation and writing of this book! Without knowing it, I must have made living a hard road to travel for them. I sincerely appreciate you all.

TABLE OF CONTENTS

Author's Note

Migration comes in two distinct ways. We have natural and forced migration.

Natural migration comes when a group of people in search of productive land for agriculture and hunting as in the old generation, or the opportunities inherent in modern technology as presently experienced in our modern world, decides to move out of ancestral land to another for survival. Usually driven by inner desires to meet human needs, man relocates willingly. Overcrowding could lead to migration. Abraham and his cousin Lot separated from each other at a particular point in life due to frictions from their respective servants. Each migrated eastward from another. At the point in question, the population of humans on earth was far smaller than available landmass. People come together to overcome the wild animals.

The Israelites migrated to Egypt at the approach of a crippling famine in the land. And they dwelt in Egypt for 430 years. The migration out of Egypt was in search of the Promise Land due to deliberate hardship and slavery conditions from their host.

In the history of man, many citizens have migrated to distant lands from their own ancestral locations due to famine, leadership afflictions and natural disasters. Animals and birds migrate seasonally, from one place to another in the quest for survival from a prevailing condition that has become precarious. The migration of Africans in the distant past was through slave trading; then with chains on their legs and necks to reduce resistance. The present migration of Africans, without chains on their legs and necks as willing offerings just to escape the rapacious activities of the leaders!

Humans do not migrate like the animals but when there is a lack of opportunities in the land, the adventurous and the strong-willed migrate to other lands in search of greener pastures. Once this dream is achieved, they return home to join in the task of family and community upgrade.

However when the leadership becomes over greedy and insensitive to the yearning of the followers, the real migration to settle permanently in other lands begins. Thus Nigeria's pathetic situation at present allows the very poor to simply watch helplessly as those who could afford the cost of migration depart their ancestral land with families. This poor segment of the society will now become the remnant of the land, not by choice, but by their evident incapacitation to escape the crippling ravages of leadership. They are left to carry the yoke of a poor managed economy.

Climatic changes and other difficulties of life hardly push the working class and the potentially working class like students to migrate!

Apart from their journey into Egypt, the Israelites, from Biblical history have dwelt in other lands, not by choice, but by force. When they depart from righteousness and begin to worship idols and other unhealthy involvements, their Creator's presence departs from their midst and other smaller nations will defeat them in wars and carry them off as slaves. This situation happened severally in their historical settlements.

African citizens migrating to other countries are caused by leadership woes. When elected and self-imposed leaders become reckless with the management of the economy due to their insatiable appetite for foreign luxury and stealing the people's wealth without conscience, the land become uninhabitable for millions to now desire migration. Corruption is the instrument of this migration perpetuated by the leaders and their cohorts against the citizens.

Any nation that allows her citizens to relocate in droves to other nations will ever remain puppets in the land of foreigners for years to come. The persecution of the Jewish population during the 2nd World war by Hitler helped them to flood America with professionals who have turned America into the policeman status of the world at present. There was economic crisis in America too, in 2007 to 2009 due to excessive mortgage lending to borrowers who did not qualify for such home loans in the Great Recession but the leadership responded carefully to that economic downturn through one relief or another. The citizens did not migrate to other lands.

Nigeria leaders see economic crisis as a battle of survival between the rich and the poor. Recently a Nigerian leader when confronted with the possibility of the country splitting into several nations replied as quoted here:

"Nigerians are too poor to revolt" He explained himself
this way, "that Nigeria cannot break up because members
of the elite are united in preserving their advantage over the
masses irrespective of their differences of tribe and religion
"Nigeria", he said, "is too weak to break. Who will break
it? Is it the ordinary person in Jigawa or the ordinary person
in Sokoto or the ordinary person in Bayelsa? Is it the Igbo
vulcanizer or the Yoruba woman selling kerosene by the roadside
or the Okada man in Delta? They don't have the capacity to unite
because they are burdened by poverty. We have taken away
from them their dignity, self-esteem, their pride and self-worth
so that they cannot even organize
"Up there, we (elite) unite.... We will never allow Nigeria to

break because once it breaks, we will lose. But the common man
loses nothing. What is he losing? He is already in hell; he cannot
lose anything more than this hell"

If leaders elected or self-imposed on the people have this mindset, salvation is very far from coming! The Holy command from the Biblical story of creation has this to say: God blessed them and said to them, "Be fruitful and increase in number, fill the earth and subdue it. Rule over the fish of the sea and the birds of the air and over every living creature that moves on the ground" (Gen1:28). The above display of the leadership mindset is not the mind created by God to undertake the Divine directives to the required level. The above utterances came from a mind warped by the corrupting tendencies of the flesh. Such a mindset will lead to Armageddon. . Our leaders are like the Queen of the ant: fat with the evidence of good living; the command soldier ants are the security protectors – the top military and police hierarchy who save-guard the leaders. Other ants that build the house and provide the food are the masses of this nation on whose shoulders the top echelon rides

CHAPTER ONE

THE GREAT MIGRATION

In the bowels of time to come, famine was to visit the earth due to man's foolishness. Nobody saw it coming. The great seers of the time could have prophesized about it but being limited to man's imperfection, they could have been limited too. Most importantly the world hardly pays attention to such prophecies until it has happened severally.

The Creator who sees the beginning and the end was aware of this visitation of hunger on mankind. Thus he planned on how to protect his chosen Inheritance from the calamity from the beginning to the end. He made ways for the children of Abraham who he had called way back in the story of creation to depart his father's land and also his people.

To make his plan succeed, he employed the foolishness in the heart of man. Among the children of Jacob, there was a hidden malevolence breeding in their hearts. The children of his first wife had hated Joseph, the first son of the second wife, Rachel out of jealousy because Jacob showed more love for Joseph than the rest. The jealousy, by this time had reached a breaking point, such that brothers from the first wife were unanimous in doing away with Joseph in whatever way possible. They were so consumed by hatred, they did not mind if he was killed. His blood on their conscience did not bother them. This is the second recorded story in creation where hatred and jealousy has led to human destruction without remorse. That of Cain and Abel was an eye opener.

The master plan of the children of Jacob to destroy Joseph fortunately had a caveat introduced. Judah became sentimental. He remembered the good side of the lad who had been bringing food and water to them in the field: nostalgia of having his blood on his conscience came up. His decision not to have Joseph's blood on his hands divided the conspiracy, selling him off to the slave traders became the best option in the immediate circumstance.

His other brothers were a little bit pacified that their common enemy would be finally taken out. Whether he was killed or sold out meant the same thing, at least their father would no longer expend his love on one child to the detriment of others.

In their mindset, a wife is a wife and their mother happened to be the senior wife of Jacob, and a senior sister to Rachel. They were not emotionally involved as their father Jacob was: they could not realize that Jacob was in love with Rachel but was forced by tradition to marry her senior sister first. They failed to see the love Jacob has for Rachel was transferred to Joseph. As members of the same family, the brothers of Joseph could not see why an issue that happened in the distant past before any of them came to be children of the same man should affect their lives. Thus to sell Joseph became a better option as Judah, their senior brother refused having Joseph's blood on their hands.

In God's plan for the preservation of his Inheritance, Joseph being the chosen seed for a new nation, and was to face the final trials in the hands of Potiphar's wife. Nothing happens in isolation unless God is not in it.

Joseph as a mortal being with limited understanding would have seen a trail of hardship: from being thrown into a pit, sold to the itinerant slave buyers and slammed into a dungeon in a foreign land because of his refusal to have canal knowledge of Potiphar's wife. And he must have prayed without ceasing to the Creator for mercy! If any man was to cry, "God why have thou forsaken me", it was Joseph. In his own grief, Jacob his father, must have seen his world collapsing as the heir-apparent has been killed by wild beast. None of his older children was seen by the beast! The agony in his mind made him age considerably within a space of time. Joseph brothers, with a new vista of hope of recognition and love staring them on the face, became suddenly aware of their father's sorrows at the disappearance of Joseph.

In God's plan, there are continuous revelations. It is a story of creation from to the end without stopping as long as the earth exists. It is God's creatures that are limited in knowledge. If man is aware that birth and death are mere processes in the equation of God's creation, certain tendencies that lead to extreme negative behavior could have been checked.

Joseph incarceration in foreign prison was the darkest point of his life; invariably the transition to his new life and role in the preservation of the chosen race though at this point in question, he didn't know it. None of his siblings and even his father Jacob knew it! That was the story of the Israelites and their sojourn in foreign land for 430 years to come.

The Exodus of the Israelites from Egypt was in God's plan, to locate them to a land flowing with milk and honey as Abraham was promised. This plan could not come into effect without a catalyst. Mankind is often bereft of positive ideas for growth but rather with complacency in thoughts and actions; he tends to relax and want to enjoy the esteemed fruit of his labor. Without a catalyst to energize him for continuous striving, he will think that he has reached the zenith of his journey on earth. It is only when appeared on the horizon more task to overcome, does mankind realize the whole truth: that in life journey, improvement is a continuous requirement in God's plan to create another heaven on earth where His reign shall be endless. Everything is destined to work out after this purpose.

Without the hardship in Egypt that started with Joseph's death, the Israelites journey into the Promise Land would still be on hold. It was the unhealthy living condition that made them remember the promise to their forefathers of a new land flowing with milk and honey.

And in this realization came the appearance of leaders and forerunners: Moses became the chosen one, made to have a royal connection which would drive out inferiority complex. Aaron was divinely positioned to act as Moses mouthpiece and the great journey recorded in history as Exodus began. God planned the mass exodus and perfected it through series of miracles and interventions that overcame the frustrations and roadblocks set up by man. Since that historic movement, other mass movements have taken place and the world is still not satisfied of mass exodus!

Be that as it may, it is worthy of note that the exodus of the Israelites from Egypt was the only divinely authorized human movement. It was cheer complacency that made them forget the plan of God upon their lives. A supposedly interim journey to dwell in a foreign land until the approaching famine cease led to many years of sit-tight in a foreign land until severe hardship worse than the famine galvanized them to remember a promise made years ago.

When Joseph was alive and many privileges came to them without struggle, the spirit of complacency set in. Until Joseph's death and a new Pharaoh came on board, the Israelites never thought of their ancestral home; they never realized that the people of Egypt were not happy to see foreigners dominate them. It is like that everywhere! None indigenes cannot dominate and rule a people in their ancestral home. God did not make mistake in locating each national in separate world map. The problem of the earth is when foreigners plan and put into action their intent to reign over another people who are grounded in their ancestral home.

England colonized many nations of the world but a time came when these nations sought freedom subtly and blatantly, which in most cases led to mass death. South African nation was ruled by foreigners, British being the top of the culprit. Over time several unpleasant policies and actions began to rear their ugly heads against the natives. There arose an uprising that could not be suppressed. Nelson Mandela became a victim of the uprising among the living. He spent 27 years of his adult life at Robben Island. But eventually the foreigners had to accept their status as visitors before peace could come to the land. Nevertheless, many souls and investments went up in flame. Foreign security and internal obstacles could not subdue the uprising. The landowners must take back their inheritance. This situation happened in Zambia, Tanzania and many African countries.

Russian ruled many nations subtly and then later with force because power emanated from Moscow;

other nations were mere visitors, used when the occasion calls for it and immediately discarded when they were no longer needed. For a very long time, this servant-master relationship thrived, until the servants felt in their bones the urgent need to free themselves. Thereafter several wars of intimidation, clandestine in nature at first and brazen in many ways ensued out of this desire for self-rule. It brought collaboration from many nations of the world, either in support or against. But with time, and massive loss of souls, Russian leaders came to the uncomfortable decision that they cannot hold other nations captive forever in their lands. Subsequently they let go their stranglehold on those nations to usher in peace and growth. These conflicts have proven to those who still hear the cautious words from their inner mind that a nation in their God given land cannot be subdued forever. The subjugation may be for a time only; the joy of freedom must come at the dawn! Otherwise the reason God created each nation differently and gave them separate landmass as theirs would be contradicted.

Having this knowledge as our background, it is with grief to note that many nations have relapsed to Stone Age status because criminals ascended the throne of leadership. The case of the African continent is a very sad and pathetic story. And it has become a free flow of shame and sorrow.

Today the citizens of these countries are wishing that the foreign colonial masters are back on the leadership positions in their countries. The reason is very simple. When the foreigners were in power, they repatriated the wealth of each nation to their countries because they invested money and human effort in the development of these colonized nations. They never syphoned these monies into private accounts because at the end of the day, they were accountable to their government. Those who performed creditably received awards and positions of respect in their land; those who performed badly ended up in prisons in their land and discriminated in the public. Honesty was a great asset.

Unfortunately when power landed in the hands of the natives, many issues never seen before when the collective agony was against the foreigners now surfaced to wrestle the new leaders to the ground. The cry of discrimination and marginalization blossomed beyond the government capacity to manage. Discrimination existed before but it was between

the foreigners and the natives; and the issue then was on qualifications and abilities to hold any position. This yardstick was never bent to favor any tribe. But power now in the hands of the indigenes threw up "son of the soil' sentiments, religious affiliations, tribal and regional colorations. Qualification took a background position in the politics of settlement. Then personal greed, suffocating as it is, came up to overshadow sincerity and accountability. The judiciary that was supposed to hold culprits to ransom became a ready and willing instrument in the hands of power brokers to manipulate for continuous and enduring evil legacies to triumph.

If the fall from grace to grass after independence had been rested on the manipulation or corrupting of the judiciary into the underdevelopment phase, it would have been less painful. What makes it greater burden is the acceptance and promotion of these criminal leaders as the best the land could offer. The reason is not farfetched. Since they lost their political power, and by far their economic stranglehold on those they ruled before due to power devolution, they still desire the economic benefits. Seeing the urgency in the new leaders to syphon ill-gotten wealth from the developing nations into their stable political atmosphere, their appetite for foreign money was assuaged. Thus once a leader emerges from the former colonies, the image launderers from the former colonial countries would submit their interest – nay to promote the image of the new leader and his cabinet members. So it is usually not strange to see the new leader and his wife receiving international awards even when they are yet to settle down to governance! And as the foreign image launderers and promoters take the next flight in and out of the country, the contractors would come in the next day with fake business documents albeit with secret windows to syphon ill-gotten wealth and dying companies in their land to repossess. Dilapidated structures would be refurbished and renovated, ready for these new leaders to buy off at exorbitant cost. This was how the first colonial masters came to the shores of African nations: first with the Bible and the Cross, then followed by the merchants with mirror, rum and gun powder.

The swindling does not end with the purchase of unenviable business structures and houses, without wasting time, vehicles the foreigners could not drive in their countries because of cost and also the airplanes are sold to the new leaders because they have realized our obsessions with foreign luxury. As good psychologist they have come to realize that Africans attach great importance to exotic cars and other luxury purchases in one's compound; the more there are these luxury items, the more rich and important the owner is regarded in the community. To increase their hold on the financial purse of the nation, many foreign universities opened their gates to accept the new leaders' offspring and also the children of the army of personal assistants. The country's scholarship board acts as a platform to offset these foreign educational bills from the nation's commonwealth. And as this swindling is going on between the criminal leaders and the previous foreign leaders, the masses' survival become acute and desperate!

The sad reality becomes the present scenario in the foreign embassies and the country's passport offices with the population of applicants growing astronomically every day because the people of the land – the landowners who had fought for political leadership from the hands of the foreigners are now desperate to willingly vacate their ancestral land and become slaves without chains around their necks in the foreigner's countries. How pathetic!

Of all the human movement from one country to another on permanent basis, nature has a standard for human relocation. The present hustle and desperation to relocate is not sanctioned by the Creator, and would in time come to regrets as the Israelites found out after 430 years in Egypt. The death of Floyd in America testifies to this assumption.

The police held Floyd who was already handcuffed by the neck with his knee, oblivious to the cry that he was suffocating until Floyd died. This was not an act on the spur of the moment to defend himself, but a script from his racial memory. To him, all non-whites are strangers who are eating up the food and other comforts he was supposed to enjoy. In his eagerness to pass judgment himself on foreigners, he overreached his official reaction to a suspect.

The way God made the world to be was each citizen of a country can interact with others on the scale of equality, using trade, marriage and work situations to create a global family. But the love of life without strife has created a sense of desperation in many peoples' mind. With criminals in power in many of the emerging nations and the greedy collusion of the ex-while colonial masters, the commonwealth is carried off beyond the reach of the masses, creating in its absent acute desperation to migrate.

The complicity of leaders to create poverty through the generations has not and will not make life comfortable for the led unless the leaders remain conscious of their responsibilities. The French revolution of 1914 was caused by absent minded leaders who jettisoned their responsibilities for absolute self-comfort. The reply from the naïve queen to the masses to eat cake instead of bread was just a catalyst to trigger the bottled up frustrations of the followers.

Today leaders in most of the developing nations remain in complacent state of life, packing the wealth of their countries' into private accounts in the developed countries of the world. And it is not that these developed nations are not aware of these financial dispossessions of the people of these developing nations. They are fully aware but cannot do anything about it. All the criticism of the few human right advocates in their midst are suppressed by the invisible power behind these financial transactions. This goes a long way to validate the old saying that, "no one is a hypocrite in his pleasure"

Many years back when slave trade was lucrative, many citizens from these developing nations were carried away forcefully into the farm settlements of South America and other developed nations as laborers. Now through the criminal activities of the leaders from these developing nations, the same cheap wealth which was represented by the slaves in the past are now transferred into the developed nations with ease through spurious projects, secretively and brazenly construed . Today sufferings and pure deprivation has made the citizens of these developing nations to seek immediate relocation into the developed nations where the expectations of the average citizen is guaranteed. To underscore the willingness of these citizens in dire need of relocation, properties and other items acquired by them over the years are sold at give-away prices just to get the visas, flight tickets and leave their native land. They are so desperate that the passport offices and the desired country's embassy to relocate are so crowded you will think there is war in their ancestral home.

Unfortunately relocation to other countries has become a struggle of the fittest. Gone are the days many citizens were forcefully carried to these nations with chains around their necks to reduce struggles, today harsh immigration laws are set out to discourage influx of other citizens from entering their land. These immigration laws can change without notice; it can become more stringent when the request for visas is on the rise. A situation has even arose where visitors with genuine visas and already airborne were denied entry on arrival in the country of choice.

Nature does not permit vacuum. It is a natural reaction that validates the old saying, "the heart of man lies where his treasure is" When, through the connivance of the developed nations, the wealth of the developing countries are clandestinely relocated out of the country, the citizens without actually seeking these wealth, would desire to relocate. For if the wealth so relocated out are used to invest in the developing nation, the citizens would not have that desire to relocate. When the wealth is relocated, its absence create such humbling situations as poor life expectancy, poor infrastructural development, unhygienic situations, educational deprivations for the offspring, health and poor living standard and other human needs not met that in the first place becomes the reasons for the migration.

The journey of the Israelites to the land of Egypt was a stop-gap measure approved by the Creator. It was sheer complacency that made them relax in Egypt for 430 years. Joseph knew that his people would not remain forever in a foreign land because before his death, he made them promise to carry his bones when leaving.

Of course the Israelites have been to other nations after their sojourn in the land of Egypt, but these movements were forced through defeat at wars. When their sins have assumed an unimaginable height in the sight of their Creator, other nations have come to defeat and scatter them.

Today aggression from one nation to another has reduced significantly otherwise the citizens of most of the developing nations whose wealth are syphoned to other nations through their criminal leaders would have been carried off as part of the spoils of war like the Israelites of old. The developed nations have only gone to war against other nations when their positions as superpowers are threatened. The U.S aggression in Iraq and Libya was specifically to silence their leaders whose radical voices of rebellion against her status as the policeman of the world were becoming strong with increasing believers/supporters. The recent aggression from Russia against Ukraine was to nip in the bud outside source of threat from their traditional political rivals

The Creator made every nation independent and provided the resources to develop and make life comfortable for its citizens. The seed of poverty and retrogression begins for each nation when their leaders become complacent and unwilling to explore the abundance in nature for growth and maturity.

These developed nations did not just wake up to a better nation. Their countries grew from rough environment to the present orderliness and provisions of the necessities of life. They grew from brigandage status, obeying laws and the attendant responsibilities for upliftment. The problem of the developing nations is their unwillingness to follow the same pathway the leaders of the developed nations passed. Having been colonized and the first indigenous leaders had their trainings and education in the land of the colonial masters, the seed of imitation and aspiration to be the new colonial masters grew in them, with the followers entrapped in the darkness of ethnic and religious folklores. There was no other challenge in them otherwise they would have aspired to create a similar environment, a semblance of sort as seen in the developed nations. The challenges encountered in the developing nations, apparently overwhelmed them.

For the a like Nigeria, the pitfalls and unwillingness to progress beyond the colonial era did not only appear in the magnitude of underdevelopment that faced the new leaders. The colonial masters' ingenuity to merge different countries together for easy control and as safety measure to dissuade other European countries from the scramble of African nations made the challenges impossible to surmount in the eyes of the emerging leaders.

If truth must be told, the British knew that the Northern Nigeria, predominantly Muslims with different approach to leadership and the Southern part cannot possibly have similar world view but because their interest was paramount, it was merged by Lord Lugard and his British interest group.

They knew that the leaders from the Northern and the Southern part of Nigeria will not readily agree on issues easily but because the divide and rule policy of the parent government favored the merger, it was allowed. Most importantly, the other European colonialist would not have strong argument during the negotiations among the Europeans on how to divide the African nations for the financial benefits thereof. And it was good crude oil had not been discovered at the time of the scramble. Otherwise it would have taken the Europeans Great War and defeat to allow the British government to possess the Nigeria contraption.

Of profound interest was the British partisan interest in the unity of Nigeria. The British government knew that if the Northern and the Southern part of Nigeria unite, then financial windfall coming to them would diminish tremendously, thus every clandestine effort was put in place to make the Northern and Southern section of Nigeria operate on different world view. The civil war – the Biafra/Nigeria civil war brought this secret politics into proper perspective.

Yes, they will readily tell whoever cares to ask that they do not desire Nigeria to disintegrate. The emerging leaders, for the selfish reason of greater financial access and control felt more comfortable with a bogus nation where financial control indices would be hard to implement based on tribal and religious sentiments which were the spring boards to corner political offices.

Overtime, these racial disjoint have metamorphosed to include greed at its worst. The average Nigeria leader considers personal empires and opportunities to consolidate his acquisition. Gradually and systematically, the wailings of the citizens and the stagnation of the country on the route to development and modernity have been muffled. The few voices of reason are soon made complacent or suffocated into silence. Corruption is evil, retrogresses not just the land but the spirit of man dwelling in the land.

Today Nigeria is in a state of disorder, like a dead elephant lying prostrate in death, with various predators feasting from it day and night, and will continue until the carcass is finished. Truth has become lies while lies have changed for truths. The citizens are giving up while the leaders are feasting nonstop on the natural benefits handed down from the Creator. Saying the truth turns you into the peoples' prime enemy. Thus while the criminals swagger about, brandishing the power of leadership, the followers wail in isolation.

It is like the world has physically and spiritually come to an end for the followers but a new vista of earth opened for the corrupt and arrogant. The years ahead will determine if falsehood will have its way eventually. It is a war between the light and darkness!

And we can verify the outcome of the last battle between darkness and light.

The daily killing of human beings and the destruction of properties tells the uninformed that darkness is winning; as if the end of life is around the corner. The dead are celebrated for escaping this terror of the day; not mourned as it was before, with the living eager to confess their iniquities for more days on the surface of the earth.

The cause of this present strife in the land is corruption, the gospel of the enemy. The colonial government could be forgiven on the condition that no one is a hypocrite in his pleasure. But to forgive our erstwhile founding fathers amount to approving the ill-foundation they laid for the generation ahead. African nations have had this bitter pill in her throat for long. It cannot be vomited or swallowed completely, with the erstwhile colonial government playing the role of witch rat.

When this bitter pill lodged itself in the throat of the Chinese rulers, the agents of light in that country quickly severed the throats of the leaders. Check it out: every nation that desired growth and upliftment of her people from the Stone Age to modernity did one spectacular task: they quickly and diligently disgorged from their system this bitter pill of corruption. Even though they were not religious like the African nations, they could recognize the satanic ministry and did everything possible to reject it.

J.J. Rawlings of Ghana recognized this insidious philosophy of the enemy and derailed its expansion with the sudden killings of corrupt and arrogant past leaders. And it brought a new vision of re-construction in the heart of every citizen of Ghana. Suddenly a country, whose citizens had scattered around the globe as Nigerians are presently doing, regrouped and fought the spirit of darkness to a standstill. Today Ghana has risen from the ashes of economic waste and unconscious indulgence during the years of pillage to a new vista of great hope.

Nigeria today is falling heedlessly into the valley of rotten bones because of corruption. While the network of roads remains death traps, the leaders – political and spiritual are worried about parking spaces for their numerous private jets. As the followers perish daily from avoidable death, diseases and hunger, the leadership budget more resources of the people to procure more jets, SUVs, bulletproof vehicles and billions of cash into private pockets for what is regarded as constituency projects!

What are these constituency projects? Are they the developments the government could not bring but now channel them through individuals? Are these constituency projects the roads that have turned to death traps, the agricultural development that have grown fitfully over the years such that Nigerians are now dependent on foreign importation of food, and many other needs of the followers? What are these projects that the government of the day could not perform effectively that would now be done by the Senators, House of Representative members, State Assembly members, Ministers, Commissioners, Director Generals of ministries and other political attachments who resemble leeches and drain pipes?

For benefit of doubt, you will not find this huge money spent in making the above needs of the people available, rather judiciously spent in providing SUVs for girlfriends, building houses for concubines, celebrating birthday's carnivals for self and concubines. The few areas they spent money providing sewing machines, motor cycles and Tricycles for transport will be celebrated with videos spread on social media. And on the day these items would be handed over to the people, a motorcade will make an entry into the community. The budget for the entertainment of the guests invited by this leader would definitely surpass the cost of the items to be shared! This constituency money finally finds its way as payment for more private jets, SUVs, security apparatus for the few elects. At the end of each year, the population's disenfranchisement increases geometrically.

People from Africa are still waiting to see apparition, black in color and with horns protruding on their foreheads from these leaders to understand their true roles as agents of satanic manifestations. The special honor and regard given to men and women of cash has made it difficult for the average man on the street to see the leader who is ensconced in profligate living as the true agent of this satanic force.

Come to Abuja in Nigeria, the seat of governance and see small underage girls involved in illicit sex and consumption. See also the growing population of young able bodied men becoming pimps and slave servants of the leaders.

The ticking of the time bomb has already started. The end of the earth is not yet approaching but the destruction of the enemies of the light has started. It may appear overwhelming at present, making the inquisitor wonder how it would come, but the wind of change has already started blowing. The history of all past civilizations can attest to this wind blowing.

When Noah began to build the Ark, the people around him were busy marrying and giving out in marriages. Like today, they would be busy purchasing more private jets, SUVs, syphoning the people's commonwealth into private pockets at the detriment of human growth and accomplishment, until like Noah, the oppressed followers gather together to be shielded by the agents of the light! Everything will seem impossible until then. Even when the people were climbing the Ark under construction to pee and poo, Noah never behaved as if he was aware until one of the cripples fell into the human excreta and got healed instantly. And Noah behaved as if he didn't notice the scramble for the human excreta by the same people until the Ark under construction became spotless, without a single stain.

The cleanliness of the Ark under construction was a miracle! And it must have compelled the inquisitor to wonder loudly on what Noah was doing. The judgment of God tarries for a time! Everyone is given the opportunity to seek the appropriate pathway for greater living. The few who wondered what Noah was into may have been persuaded to conclude that Noah might be mad after all.

For us in Africa, the feasting is increasing in private abodes across the length and breadth of the country while the wailings of the oppressed can be heard loudly along the streets. They are congregating gradually around the eagle's square. And by the time they gather fully, the police, the army and every other agent of the leadership would be overcrowded into submission. The leaders would finally drag themselves painfully out from the overladen tables of consumption to enquire the reason for the gathering of the magnitude of the citizens!

CHAPTER TWO

The Destruction of
the Nation

From the outset, the nation Nigeria was not planned to succeed. The country was made up of people with divergent world view, which correctly placed them into several different nations.

The colonial masters knew this fact very well but because of selfish interest, they refused to thread this pathway of honor. Firstly, the colonialists were always against agitation for self-rule. They ever desired the colonized to see them as god sent, almost equivalent to the Creator. Thus whatever decision and agreement arrived at UK must be abided by the natives. Any sign of rejection in part or full were never tolerated by the government of the time. Blackman, they have concluded, have no brain to reason for self; he cannot govern his people. In their mindset, God specifically appointed them to rule over the Dark Continent. It follows then that as the wind of self-rule blew across Africa, the colonial masters were at an edge, angry and bitter with the few advocates of self-rule in the nation. Naturally humans have this pathological attitude of not wanting their successors to do better. Thus a departing leader, especially if forced out, naturally desires to bury minefield along the pathway of an incoming leader just to prove to the gullible masses that God approved his poor leadership. The colonial master only thought on how to perpetuate their leadership through agents who must come from the natives. Thus the self-rule agitators became the perfect instrument to mold for leadership perfection.

The scramble for the soul of the continent was staked on the basis of country by country. In a display of a pre-meditated plan, the British quickly connives among themselves to drag different nations together under one umbrella called Nigeria. At the table of negotiation among the European nations, the British colonial masters would present a country called Nigeria, politically overruling any disagreement from any other country, most importantly as the policeman of the world at the time Nigeria was birthed on fraud: to gather all the profit of colonizing many countries as one entity, reducing in the process the logistics and the challenges thereof in managing many separate nations individually.

The British knew very well that the Northern and Southern Nigeria world views are nearly parallel except perhaps on economic approach. The rich and the powerful in the North believes that it was Allah that appointed them to their positions of importance and thus, the followers must not go to school, must not possess anything materially, must be herded like sheep spiritually. They will only eat the leftovers from their overladen tables; the children of the rich must rule over the followers in perpetuity. The rich are the aristocrats while the followers are the commoners. Unlike the Southern part where everyone is a king unto himself: free to navigate the thoroughfare of life. The colonial leadership was fully conscious of this great divide.

The psychology of man does not approve his irrelevance in life. Even when he is deficient in knowledge, scarce in good health and has retrogressive approach to world growth pattern, the soul of man continues to grapple with relevance. Until God approves his departure from the surface of the earth, no man desires to be dumped into irrelevance. Even at the peak of his struggle to remain relevant, the mortal man would be ready to collapse nature just to prove that he is still relevant.

The colonial leadership was aware of this human trait, but deliberately chose the unenviable pathway that brought these nations into one entity called Nigeria. And they went further to stifle any opinion contrary to their master plan.

Overtime it became a lie that must be protected at any cost. The next leadership from the natives was made to see the indivisibility of the Nigeria as a cross to carry and hold firm. It became like the Ark of God in the land of the Jews.

Many things, like cobweb were introduced or permitted for the new leaders as a way to keep a stranglehold on the nation by the colonial masters. Many illegal doors of opportunities were opened for the new leaders: to buy properties abroad; to process and manage foreign bank accounts where the wealth of the developing nations are hidden without interference. Knowing the African appetite for foreign luxuries, the sales of obsolete and near modern technologies broadened without limit just to control the economy of nations previously under their rule.

It was no longer the slave and agricultural products that created an industrial explosion in Europe, the window of illegal privileges granted the new leaders from Africa ensured that more resources flows into Europe through the sales of obsolete equipment, deposition of stolen wealth, buying of properties and improving the general wellbeing of the children and grandchildren of the colonial masters. Do you know that when a thieving leader from Africa buys a house in Europe, he engages the services of gardeners, plumbers, maintenance crew? These workers are paid the statutory salary of citizens from that country whereas his returnee of staff at home receive very degrading peanuts as salary from the leader, sometimes never paid for months without end, yet the worker is expected to be happy for the honor to serve   the leader. The salary of a simple house gardener overseas surpasses the collective salaries of his household servants in his country. Do you know that our leaders setting up industries abroad ensures the wellbeing of the children and grandchildren of his former colonial overlords while people in his native country where he pillages the commonwealth like a rascal sleep the night over on empty stomach? Do you wonder why public and private installations are harvested overnight in the developing countries? By taking what belongs to the citizens overseas, and with the connivance of the foreign leaders, would it not amount to double tragedy when these foreign leaders begin to checkmate the owners of this wealth using strange and stiffer immigration laws when they come knocking at the door?

There is no falsehood in nature. When the hunter learns to shoot without missing, the birds would learn how to fly without perching. Repatriate all the money hidden in Western banks and investment houses from African leaders; Close other avenues for illegal fund transfer from Africa, property sales abroad will crash like stock market, foreign schools will close; most industries that depend on raw materials from Africa will shut down. If this is done, African nations will bounce back to prosperity; strife, killings and other atrocities of the present day will cease. The war instruments are produced by developed nations and sold to African nations to keep them perpetually at war so they will ever remain busy while the plunder of their country continue unabated. When the above mentioned demands are met, immigration laws would be relaxed and even money would be added as incentives for willing immigrants but no one will be willing to relocate abroad again. Those who are already there would be making plans to return!

The camouflage and secrecy surrounding the leaders' personal wealth in their former colonial countries, for Nigeria, proves beyond argument that the initial agenda behind the amalgamation of Northern and Southern segment of different nations into one entity called Nigeria is still relevant and the inability to break this yoke of servitude through the leadership very strong. No Nigeria leader at present ever thinks of dividing the country because of his personal interest. The bigger the country remains, the easier it is to corner illegal wealth at the expense of the looming population.

Today the leaders' offspring are well ensconced in foreign countries where their father's wealth are locked up in banks, properties and investment platforms; they maintain great distances from the strife engulfing their fatherland because of the unrelenting retrogressive actions of their fathers and the connivance of the colonial masters.

It is certainly very sad to witness the still birth of the lofty dreams and aspirations of the citizens of this great nation at independence in 1960. In the race to amalgamate the Northern and Southern segment of the contraption called Nigeria, the colonial masters set other agenda in place to frustrate any chance of unity among the nations. They knew that the world could change if the new leaders decided to drop all hold points to effective relationship and design a better pathway for growth.

First they set the North on the terrain of high superiority with their counterpart in the South. When they could not penetrate the North's religious barriers as it was easier in the South, they created a wall of resistance like the Berlin Wall of Germany between the North and the Southern part of Nigeria, thus erecting a gulf of mistrust through religious intolerance and ethnic segregation.

Misplaced priorities were handed over to the leaders in Africa like the Ten Commandments given to Moses. When Nigerian leaders return from oversea trips, you will think their next step would be to replicate what they saw abroad. No, the opposite is what comes to the citizens. Their travelling overseas deprives the citizen of great wealth because they will be involved in numerous parties, economic meetings for more pillaging of the commonwealth, and other miscellaneous wastages; When they return from such irrelevant trips, the citizens are deprived further through 'estacode' payments, entourage waste of resources from airport to government house; more hardship through sudden and impromptu policies usually from monetary lenders across Europe, designed to improve the revenue base of the government for more pilfering opportunities.

Switzerland is known in financial circle as a heaven for illegal wealth holding nation through her banking system. Thus every kind of wealth: espionage related wealth, stolen wealth from leaders around the world, financial heist from criminal. All the actors in shadowy business feel comfortable when the proceeds of their actions are lodged in Swiss bank.

For developing nations, however Paris, UK, America, Dubai, Canada and other top European nations holds the status of financial heaven for past and present leaders. Nigeria's obsession with UK is second to none. As soon as they ascend onto power, medical treatment and schooling for self and children will start. Buying of properties, starting with houses will follow up immediately. Once they have secured homes abroad, the stealing spree of the people's commonwealth will start. The citizen become poorer by the time they leave office for other dream merchants.

Obi Pascal (not his real name) was a lawyer. When he became a governor, the gardeners in his son's house abroad were paid more than teachers in the state his father governed. While the gardeners received their pay regularly, the teachers in his father's domain were not paid regularly, and when they protested for lack of regular payment, the governor sacked them over the television. And to demonstrate his carefree attitude to the followers, when his wife died, he buried her with raw cash in the same coffin. Thank God, the thieves arrived in the middle of the night to retrieve the coffin and took all the jewelries and the money buried with the dead.

Incidentally Obi Pascal was perceived as one of the best governor to have walked through the Nigeria land space. The mindset of the leaders is anti-development but the attitude of the followers is what has condemned us as citizens for choosing darkness instead of light!

At one point in time, a top leader of the government in charge of communication openly stated that telephone usage is not for everyone.. This man later spent about 12 years or more in the hallowed chamber of the Senate passing laws for the country. His deficient mentality did not foresee the appearance of cellphone of the present day. When a blind man is in charge! Another governor arrogantly stated that education is not for everybody. That week, he celebrated his son's graduation from a foreign university. And he has a private university where automatically he is the Chancellor! Apparently he is grooming his children to take over leadership in Nigeria because while he and his cohorts made sure that education does not work in Nigeria, his children and other children of the elites graduate from foreign universities. In the not distant future, one of his children would be appointed the Vice Chancellor of his university, just as the children of the General Overseers of today Pentecostal churches nominate their own children as the next General Overseers in their Churches.

Thank God that our leaders have no hand on the key to human survival. The road to Heaven, we are told, is never straight or paved with gold. It is a minefield strewn with thorns. Yet the Nigerians surviving the hardship inflicted on them by their leader's criminal attitudes signify their own journey of life through the heavenly pathway, the narrow route!

Today many Nigerian citizens are in foreign prisons in their quest for survival against the harsh realities of staying in their father's land while leaders, elected or imposed remain perfectly well in slumber, celebrating inanities like children's marriages, birthday carnivals for self and concubines, burial ceremonies and other such vain gatherings of the elites hugely meant to declare abundance in the things of the flesh. Strangely they always invite the clergy to pray and bless their gatherings. The Beatitudes of Jesus Christ on the mountain is not for our leaders. Jesus Christ said: "Blessed are the meek, for they will inherit the earth"; "Blessed are those who hunger and thirst for righteousness, for they will be filled; "Blessed are the merciful, for they will be shown mercy" Our leaders are not merciful, they are not after righteousness neither are they meek but arrogant. The rush to acquire the bounties of the earth is their belief that they will own this earth!

Insecurity of life and properties has risen to the level of epidemic. Kidnapping and terrorism have increased in geometric dimension in our land. It is now very clear, even for the most skeptics that satanic forces are now in firm control of the Nigeria space. Young children who are supposed to be in school challenging the opinions and decisions of the past generation for a new earth, have deviated into criminal trenches for ritualism, pool betting arena, forever waiting for instant wealth. Desperation in life does not bring peace but chaos.

Once upon a time, a Senate President was disgraced out of his office for collecting bribe so he can increase the yearly educational budget. What a crime against the wellbeing of the future generations! And while he was at this powerful position of life and the opportunity to effect positively or otherwise the budget of a ministry, his offspring were in foreign land, either in schools or just living it off big with Nigeria's wealth.

The captivity of Israelites by Nebuchadnezzar and other leaders in the bible story started like Nigeria present crises. We are now in the throes of captivity, this time not by powerful leaders from outside Nigeria space but by our own leaders' collusions with internal and external agents of retrogression. It is now very acceptable to review our journey of life as a nation. And we can vividly recollect a time in the distant past when Africans wailed piteously , with chains of servitude around their necks and legs as they were transported forcefully into foreign lands as slaves, to work for the economic growth of the foreign countries. Yes, that was in the distant past but the trend has not stopped despite the abolition of slave trade several years ago. Africans are today selling their little possessions and relocating to foreign countries for survival despite the avalanche of mineral deposits in their own country.

It is an open secret now to hear that foreigners now come into Nigeria and freely and boldly harvest these deposits of minerals in the land. In Nigeria, vested interest groups among our leaders sponsor terrorists to dislodge communities with mineral deposits, and then the harvest begins. The Chinese come with chartered helicopters and land in such community after a makeshift living and working conditions have been provided after the sacking of the indigenes by bandits. Has anyone wondered why criminals would enter an area, sack the land dwellers easily like that and the government unable to stop the mayhem despite the heavy budget for security every year? Fat security budget/allowances for each state are not to provide security but to instigate more security challenges. For instance, there was a period the government gave open cheques book to a state government to ensure proper security in the state, to reduce the incessant security challenges in the oil and gas business environment. The leaders at the state level and with their cohorts outside the state made money with ease. They saw it as repatriation of fund meant for the oil bearing lands in the state which the federal government was denying the state. Of course the security crisis reduced tremendously, but once the federal government withdrew the open cheques, the security crisis will increase overnight. The kidnapping and ransom payment, the destruction of installations and the pirate activities will multiply suddenly. The environment would become very unsafe to navigate; oil and gas   production will decline. The country's revenue base will plummet downwards. Once this crisis comes up, the group involved in oil bunkering will be counting of poor business period, the foreign vessels used by our leaders will avoid Nigeria waters like a plague, free money to harvest will reduce, but most importantly, the leaders will lack money to syphon abroad; foreign trips for celebration of inanities will be on pause mode. However when the leaders' dependents, their concubines, and other vested interest groups who have latched themselves to the leaders begin to get upset and bitter, the open cheques is once more released for security reasons.

The war among the various interest groups to hijack the wealth of the nation is more ferocious than the pursuit of wild lions. In Nigeria, the oil and gas industry is owned and operated by foreign economic powers. If you see any company owned by a Nigerian, the foreign powers are not far at the back, remotely pivoting the activities in the field. The presence of the Nigerian crew in the setup is to wade off antagonism from the citizens and also to reduce operational cost as the Nigerian factor would come into play: availability of cheap labor without grudges.

Take the Akpo field for a clearer understanding. The pipeline was laid by Saipem. The Saipem FDS1, owned by the French and Italia governments, was the barge that did the pipe laying. Total Nigeria Limited awarded this contract to Saipem. As a company policy, Saipem does not enter the country of operation through the country's water route. They come in through a neighboring nation for easy settlement. While the citizens of the country of operation remain in the town awaiting the arrival of the barge, the vessel is already in the deep sea, carrying out the preliminary vital activities for vessel stabilization, other important deep sea installations before the pipe laying activity begins. These initial activities take up to 3 months daily work regime to complete.

The security and immigration departments are fully aware of these happenings but they hardly do anything to avoid the shortcut. The immigration officials collect foreigners passports, come to the offices in the town and duly process them; and stamp them. The Navy patrols the vicinity of this area to guarantee security. The Saipem office in Port Harcourt, using a contractor, begins to arrange Nigerians for the work, not the key workers but the casual low paying calibers. The Quality control workers whose expertise does not contradict the ways and manners of the key workers would be deployed first and finally the pipe coating workforce because the job slot favors Nigerians. It will cost Saipem's management great amount of money in salary and logistics if the pipe coating crew are deployed from Asia.

For private pockets, Nigeria leaders have sold the destiny of their offspring cheaply to foreign slave traders. The leaders behave as if one day, when their own children have finished schooling abroad, they will simply come back and take over leadership positions from all the foreign establishments operating in Nigeria. Years of Apartheid in South Africa was due to foreign investment, which cost that country massive blood flow like a river. A story had it that a Nigerian with an oil well went to an American university and built an office block for the school. His reasons were two-fold: to place his name on the honor list of the school and to show appreciation because his two daughters graduated from the school. Yet in his native land, children were still begging for food on daily basis as almajiris, still sharing dirty waters with cows; and still dying of preventable diseases and other challenges of growing up in a poverty ravaged society.

Be that as it may, it was not only in Nigeria, and in the execution of Total Nigeria Limited project that Saipem operated this philosophy of entering the country of project execution through another nation's water ways. In Angola Deep Sea pipe laying activity, Saipem passed through the Republic of Congo. It was only at the Mediterranean Sea that they could not navigate through another waterway. And they lost the services of many Asian workers who see the barge as a refuge. But in other porous African nations Saipem must pass through a neighboring country for better financial gain.

As the Akpo project progressed, everything Saipem needed for comfort came from Cameroun. Even the flight bringing workers must land in Cameroun; hotels in Cameroun were on a tight booking because workers must spend a day or two before the sea journey to project site in Nigeria, the same way departing workers spent days in Cameroun, first to heal from the sea sickness before the flight homeward become possible. Every food item, from water to toiletries came from Cameroun. The land of Cameroun benefited more from a project executed in Nigeria. Despite the fact that it takes less than 8 hours to reach Port Harcourt from project site, Saipem foreign workers endured the turbulent sea from project site to Cameroun for 21 hours duration which was slightly reduced to 18 hours with Surfer Sea going vessels came to their rescue.

The wealth that was supposed to enter the Nigeria space for better upliftment of her citizens ended up in other neighboring nations. What a foundation for generations to come because of this wrong philosophy of satisfying private pocket and the mentality that 'if I don't do it, another will do it and become better'! Can you cut your nose to spite your face?

The Akpo platform was constructed in faraway South Korean. The South Korean women did the painting of the platform. And the project took more than 3 years to complete. Even at that, foreign workforce were in control of the work activities till Nigerian workers started coming in trickles. The Installation activities were handled by a father and his son as back to back workforce. Thus whatever was wrongly installed by the father cannot be altered by the son, and vice versa. Project integrity cannot be questioned! Whatever is presented for public scrutiny has been vetted and approved by interest parties.

A sad history, you'll say! Total is a foreign company, Saipem is another foreign company. The platform was fabricated in South Korea. South Africa workers virtually supervised every activity on the barge. All the supporting barges were owned and managed by foreigners. The few Nigerians that participated in those projects were like stray cats; they were made to obey the rules and not to oppose any. Whatever that was wrong were not expected to come to the surface.

Mongo Park discovered the River Niger in Nigeria and became a study material in the history of discoveries despite the fact that River Niger has being in the same place for ages before the arrival of the Portuguese sailors, so also the wealth of African nations find their way into foreign countries because African leadership is embroiled in selfishness, greed, pride and material lordship. As the first European merchants entered African domain with mirror, rum and gun powder for the chiefs in exchange for agricultural products and slaves so the present leaders in Africa, especially Nigeria are crowded with investment opportunities in foreign lands, secret banks for hiding of stolen wealth, foreign made SUVs, airplanes, sea going Yatch, foreign women, oversea universities for offspring, health treatment opportunities, and what's more: the conducive peaceful environment to enjoy their loot.

The devastation created in most of these African nations by wanton looting of resources, and deprivation of opportunities for the growing population cannot be solved by political or economic platitudes by the leaders and their cohorts in foreign lands. And the years of hardship cannot deter any people willing to navigate the freedom pathway. It surprises an inquisitive mind when foreign countries' immigration laws begin to be stiffer to discourage immigration of other nationals when the same laws were not made stiffer to reject foreign money deposited into their banks, property purchases and industries by present and past leaders from other nations. It amounts to the greatest betrayal of man to man. A big parchment of shame on mankind: we come into the earth empty handed, struggled to possess everything needed or not, then leaves the earth empty handed but the crises we created may never varnish from the earth from one generation to another.

Africa is a gold mine of the earth. Years of resource pilfering from within and from outside cannot limit the growing trend for freedom from hegemonic agents of the devil. 'Blessed are the meek, for they will inherit the earth'.

The story of the earth has never changed and it is not going to change fast until the appointed time. This time has not been revealed to man! However, it is rather strange trying to gauge the mindset of African leaders. Their journey on the corridors of power is shamefully predictable. It is very difficult to obtain 10 leaders out of 100 on acceptable roadmap. All the preaching in the churches and mosques scattered at every nook and cranny of this nation means nothing to the working of their minds. As soon as they climb unto power, waste of resources on pleasures: eating habit and harem of women becomes their immediate occupation.

What Walter Rodney wrote several years ago, specifically in 1972 on "How Europe Underdeveloped Africa" is still not only prevalent but pervasive in Africa of today. The author acknowledged that the 'trade in slaves was facilitated by African rulers' greed for luxury goods and European products' The Japanese and the Chinese went overseas to learn their secret of dominations on many items of trade, returned to their fatherland to produce same items on higher standard or as cheaper alternatives. The Africans went overseas to buy properties, stack their money in secret banks and display abundant riches like the oil rich Saudi Arabian princes through continuous looting of commonwealth.

Today the African rulers are no longer stealing in slave trade directly but as indirect trade. By looting the treasury with reckless abandon and spending the money on luxury items like SUVs, airplanes, owning properties abroad and generally selling off the job opportunities as it is currently found in the oil and gas, the citizens are crowded with bleak future. Thus without putting chains on their necks and legs, the citizens willingly offer themselves as slaves to foreign countries. Take a walk to most embassies in Nigeria and you will think Nigeria is in a war situation, with nearly everybody eager to get out before the conflagration consumes them.

J. J. Rawlings of Ghana tried to salvage this unwholesome despicable situation in Ghana in the past by killing past leaders of that country. At the time in question, Ghanaians were in situations most pathetic as Nigeria is at present, each person desperate and eager to create a safe distance between himself and the fatherland, Ghana. They flooded every country on earth, like rattlesnakes, looking for the barest means of survival. It was very pathetic for the citizens of Ghana.

In those days, Nigerian men used the Ghanaians to learn how to have sex. Then with a little naira in your possession, fresh virgins and near virgins from Ghana: a set of uncomplicated womanhood would be offered like lambs on the altar of sexually starved Nigerians

But J. J. Rawlings came after much notification through threats to an uncaring bunch of leaders. Against a mountain of insincere pleadings from other evil leaders from around the world, siting fundamental human rights, he gathered them and quickened their journey to the great beyond. Suddenly sanity returned to the leadership and Ghana reversed their journey into the valley of history.

It is a wonder that Nigeria, having benefited from that history of near hopelessness of a next door neighbor, would mindlessly thread that same pathway of shame and human desperation. Truly nothing is new on the face of the earth. Man's inability to learn from history has been the underlying factor in human struggle on earth. This present migration of Nigerians into all the nooks and crannies of the earth didn't start today; rather desperation has heightened its occurrence. It is a migration of the fittest, caused by an approaching terror of death; it is not the seasonal migration of animals.

In the late 60s, in the twilight of the end of the civil war between Biafra and Nigeria, many Biafra's families were torn apart with fear and dread of imminent death. Acute hunger, orchestrated by Nigeria to weaken the strength of the emerging nation called Biafra, turned every citizen into a desperate animal hungry for food. Malnutrition and Kwashiorkor have already ravaged the populace to a point of wishing for the merciful hands of death, but the possibility of the Nigerian troop overrunning the Biafra land brought unimaginable terror in the minds of the citizens such that every family desired one or two of their children to join the Caritas plane into Gabon. The story of evil manifested by the Nigerian troops on taking over any segment of Biafra land was never appealing! The shooting of male children, the rape of women, young and old created a holocaust in the minds of the surviving Biafrans. Thus everybody, mostly the highly connected made sure that one or two of their children joined the mass exodus of young Biafrans to Gabon.

The food crisis turned everybody into a beggar. While the adults ate anything on the face of Biafra land like lizard and snakes, the most vulnerable group - the children descended into severe lack and malnutrition. Kwashiorkor became like epidemic, afflicting all and sundry. The food brought around by the Caritas planes were hijacked by the strong and powerful even at that crisis point. It was this hijacking of available food that compelled the authorities in Gabon to request the Caritas plane to return after each delivery of food with dozens of small children ravaged by hunger, sickness and malnutrition.

The unspoken consensus among the Biafra parents at that level of deprivation was that if the Nigerian military eliminates every person once they succeeded in overcoming the Biafran soldiers' resistance, at least a remnant of that enclave called Biafra land will be available to write the narrative without prejudice. It was an exodus made possible by the approaching danger to life.

The present exodus of Nigerians from their father's land is made possible by the approaching danger to life occasioned by kidnapping, terrorism and Leadership's mountain of sins. And like in any other sphere of human struggles, only the well to do can afford the cost of this mass exodus. The man on the street struggling to have a semblance of a meal in a day does not dream of relocating outside the country. Those who have properties like land, houses or cars dispose these items once the visa is approved. Like the hunger that ravaged the land of Biafra, the children of the leaders and the well-connected never suffered malnutrition and Kwashiorkor. It was the humanitarian spirit of the Caritas team that made most of the sick and the malnourished to travel to Gabon.

The Israelites migration to Egypt was caused by the approaching famine in the land. It was brought about by weather changes, not leadership sins and deprivations. The rains became scarce, ushering in drought never seen on earth before. Due to the influence of River Nile and the entrepreneurship of the Egyptians, the land was better prepared to withstand the impending hunger in the world. The Creator already made plans for the survival of his chosen race through the sale of Joseph.

Check the history of this earth. Usually it is those little happenings that generate earth shaking events, like the tiny mustard seed that became the mightiest tree in the land. But while it starts without notice, the simple minded would remain aloof until it became devastating. When the drumbeat of war begins to sound from a tiny group in the society, the generality of the populace will go about their lives untroubled. When this drumbeat is beaten by the few percentage of the populace who masquerade about as leaders but with the mass media and a band of ignorant supporters whose main drive is the appealing laden table of the leaders, know it then that the evil wind of destruction will not be far in approaching. When the leaders who have internal war among themselves over the sharing formula of the spoils of office begin the war of attrition, the simple minded who neither are aware of the issue at stake nor will be opportune to partake will face their daily life of struggle for survival. This standoff attitude changes immediately a loved one returns home in a body bag. Then you will see a massive population of the fathers, youths and even mothers very willing to put on the battle dress without formal training.

I have a Godson, like Simeon in the Bible; the child was handed over to me at baptism. Few days back, the father told me that my son, Mike with his siblings, will be relocating to Canada where their mother was already schooling and working. I turned and went into their house to see the kids. I was happy outwardly but grief stricken in my heart. The leadership malady and its associated consequences have finally landed at my door step. Like other families I knew who relocated abroad, we are about to lose these beautiful kids to other countries. I was very sad as I look at Mike's face. My spiritual son's parents are on the upscale of the society. The father is a medical doctor but the insecurity in the land and the economic valley our leaders have dragged us into does not give him the hope that his children will do better than him by remaining in the country. Now he will go to Canada and slave for another country, just like other professionals who have relocated abroad since. But this is a country whose citizens still die from preventable diseases. His services are needed in Nigeria like never before, not abroad.

I was very sad indeed. The only thing that made me smile and applaud the journey was after my inner reflections on Nigeria continuous descent into the valley of hopelessness. Two weeks to this information about my son relocating abroad, he has been sleeping the nights without electricity. The reason summarizes the fate of Nigeria in the hands of blind pathfinders who swagger about as leaders. The transformer attached to their residence was vandalized by thieves in the thick of the night because there was no light to it. The distribution company has not even woken from slumber to pass blames to the consumers for not providing security for the transformer, which automatically commands the community to start planning for replacement. Thus it was better for Mike and other children of citizens who have the resources to relocate abroad where light in the day and nights are seen to be same light!

CHAPTER THREE

The Herald of 'Japa' philosophy

When Israel went into Egypt, they were very few in number, just the children of Jacob. And it was at the approach of famine in the land. When they stayed at Egypt the population increased tremendously such that the Egyptians became afraid that visitors may rise up one day and attack them in their ancestral land. The fear of being driven out of their land became a worry that gave them nightmares but they were constrained to speak out because of Joseph's influence in Egypt.

However at the death of Joseph and the arrival of a new Pharaoh, who perhaps had been sharing the fears of the Egyptians, the fears began to take solid form in human expression. By the time Moses was born, the instruction from the Egyptian rulers to kill every male child born to the Israelites has been in force. History did not record the number of children born to the Israelites and killed by the Egyptians before the exodus.

But the journey to Egypt started at the approach of a devastating famine; still 430 years dwelling in Egypt could not guarantee the status of indigenes, showing a Divine reason for locating each citizen in a land of their own.

Today Nigerians are leaving their fatherland in droves to other countries on the surface of the earth in search of better life prospects. This movement called 'JAPA' is not driven by an approaching natural disaster like famine but man-made difficulties orchestrated by agents of hardship. In the land they are running into, there are no electricity problems, no bad roads, and no impure water for citizens to drink! All these evidences of true and real development made possible by other human beings whose brains were not anti-progress!. The air space is regulated for safety by the government, not where every Dick and Harry purchases second-hand airplanes to navigate in. The food availability and balance is very high; citizens spend less on food because farming is encouraged, mechanized agriculture at that, definitely not where business groups collect loans meant for agriculture to import low quality goods from around the globe. The government is fully determined to provide food for the masses; they do not import every of their foodstuff from abroad. Every care and energy is spent on food production and availability, not where government officials encourage the masses to patronize local products while the next approaching airplanes carry theirs into the country.

And most importantly the health matters of the citizens are placed into dedicated and professional hands, with considerable resources provided in the yearly budget for improvement. It is not a section where the minister and other health management workers shares huge slice of the budget at the end of the year as unspent fund, yet with many citizens abandoned at every hospital for lack of drugs and a motivated workforce. It is also not a section where citizens are left to carry their crosses with hospitals and clinics inadequately provided to even treat an ordinary dog while the leaders navigate in and out of foreign hospitals for common headache and at government expenses.

Overseas, children hardly know the word 'darkness' as the Sun in the day and light in the night are similar in appearance to their senses. Even in extreme poverty, children abroad hardly see darkness around them. Thus by taking our children to these environments, the future population that will move the nation forward to high level of development has gone. Thus Nigeria will continue to bring in foreigners into the country to harvest the abundant minerals in her land. Whether these imported foreign workers are Nigerians, their homes abroad remains their natural homes; and we may be compelled to settle their bills in foreign currencies as they have become citizens of another country. Already this act of importing workers from abroad has started with our leaders bringing their offspring who graduated from foreign universities to manage very sensitive positions in government.

The road network in the country is purely death traps, majorly allowed to exist by the leaders since hunger and other deprivations could not help to reduce the population. The SUVs imported by these leaders are used to navigate the small stretch of roads from their amoral hunting grounds to offices or residences daily. Long distance journeys are made with private airplanes. At present virtually every Senator and House of Representative members have private airplanes packed at designated spots meant for the rich at the nation's local and international airports. Since we have 109 Senators, 360 House of Rep members, the populations of airplanes have come to above 400. Airplane has become a status symbol! When you add the Presidential fleet close to 20 and the 36 State Governors, the statistic increases! Add also 2 or 3 airplanes for General Overseers (my God is not a poor God) of each Pentecostal church spread at every nook and cranny like the octopus in the country, then the businessmen and women in the country, we can safely agree that private planes in the country is close to a million in number. This is a country that is virtually at the bottom of the poverty signpost of the   world.

The above population of private airplane owners is the greatest parasite on the economy. If you go deeper, they are the real agents of retrogression in the nation! The politicians and the religious group are like witch rats; they eat your flesh while blowing breeze. Any country seeking true development does not encourage the growth of this group.

Every year impressive budget is presented with lots of official enthusiasm but which ends up in private pockets to service these channels of waste. The recent financial sleaze in Humanitarian department was enough sign that the nation has entered an evil hole. Do you know that Covid-19 palliative contributed by nations on humanitarian ground was hidden from the people by leaders, pending when they will go out on political campaigns or when they will celebrate birthdays!. If they can transfer money meant to help the terrorist and banditry displaced citizens into private accounts of cronies in the government of the day, the trillions in the budget will also disappear. And when the money is not in the treasury of Nigeria, the leaders quickly call the World Bank, the I.M.F and other lenders from Europe and America for loans. As always, the Chinese and the Islamic banks are around the corner with the requested loans. The oil, gas other mineral deposits are there to guarantee payback. Some of the money so borrowed is used to service the loans. None of the leader, even those sleeping on the floor of the Senate and House of Reps pavilion after sessions of full workout with energetic little girls younger than their children, would welcome the slightest reduction of waste they accumulates per month as if the Nigeria masses are sacrifices for their enjoyment. Of course when they die after years of over indulgence, the commonwealth is depleted further to accomplish a triumphant journey back to the Creator. They must go back like royalty!

The health challenges of the earth dwellers is increasing daily due to lifestyle changes, thus careers in health is on the rise and many Africans migrating overseas easily get work with trainings in health care delivery. Today the education of African children is overtly directed into the healthcare sector for easy procurement of visas and easy access to work once they are relocated. Apart from a handful in the ICT sector, majority are now into the healthcare sector, even at the breeding grounds in Africa.

In Nigeria and other African nations, the healthcare sector, is from all intents and purposes a wilderness, retrogressing yearly as more challenges come into play. The leaders and their offspring can access foreign hospitals. Even past leaders are constitutionally empowered to access foreign hospitals severally at government expenses despite the volume of illicit wealth in their possession.

With these scenarios of jungle living before us, can anyone have the moral courage to dissuade anyone from migrating? Except the leaders who preach such gospel anytime they wake up from slumber and realize that pretty soon the population of servants at their beck and call has diminished. It is always a nightmare when suddenly they wake up to give instructions and the servants before their presence reduce further in population. Like the Egyptians who woke up one day without the multitude of Israelites at the mercy of their instructions and horsewhip, the elites in Nigeria wakeup with cold sweat on their brow to witness more reduction of the servants population. But apart from preaching their evil gospel against migration, they still find it very hard to forsake indulgence and wastage of commonwealth for the sake of the less privileged in their midst.

What is there for celebration? The most High God gave us crude oil to harness and provide succor for other African nations around us but deliberately we decided to establish refineries outside the shores of this nation. We are now compelled to import finished products into the country. The government of the day is aware of this issue; the World Bank and IMF eggheads are in the know. The government also knew there was no subsidy in the first place, even as NNPC monopolizes the importation of these finished products. At less than 200 naira per liter of PMS, The sole importer was making plenty gain. The subsidy theory was a calculated fraud aimed to disenfranchise the citizens of this nation by a small clique of powerful Nigerians in positions of trust.

Instead of the government to go after this group living fat on the sweat of the people, they quickly increased the pump price of the commodities to appease the World Bank, the IMF and the oil majors who had been crying that the little percent of crude oil set aside for domestic consumption must be debited to the country at international price. The crude oil theft in the nations by known but powerful individuals left the oil majors asking the country to buy at international bench mark so they can recover cost of investment. At the moment, the manifold consequences are sending the vulnerable citizens prematurely to the grave while the leaders are busy celebrating birthdays and great achievements with the arrival of their custom-built airplanes.

Not too long ago, we spent 16 billion dollars on electricity upgrade in the country. We turned few individuals into millionaires overnight but we harvested more darkness for the populace. Many panels were set up by the government, but it ended as a jamboree. Today the government has increased tariff on electricity to pacify the World Bank and IMF eggheads. The Generating, Transmitting and Distribution companies in the electricity sector are the leaders masquerading as investors.

Whenever I sit down to analyze and quantify the colossal damage and retrogression brought about by corruption to the people of Nigeria, and also the lack of hope on ground like a sore thumb, I feel so bad and depressed that I will be asking God to approve my departure from the surface of the earth, for if other people are asking for more days on the surface of the earth, most Nigerians are not asking for such except the leaders who would naturally be crying when they hear of death.

As it stands now, many Nigerians would be eager to change places with other nationalities despite the mountain of natural deposits of minerals in the country. What is there to celebrate? We bring out from the bowel of the earth, at a minimal cost of operation, crude oil. All we need to do is to refine this product for other nations to buy direct from us. If this is done, job for the citizens will be surplus, the economy will be at its peak; foreigners would come crawling for jobs . But no, the leaders' mindsets are different. Their lack of vision for growth militated against this noble idea. They came up with the idea of buying finished products from countries that had no crude oil deposits like Nigeria because they established refineries abroad and by mutual consent among themselves sold all the jobs to foreigners

Thus when you mention the real enemies of progress of this nation, they are not the foreigners because if the house rat did not tell the visiting rat there is fish in the house, the visiting rat will never know. The leaders are the true enemies of this nation, not the cybercrime/internet operator who found the job out of frustration to exist in a warped environment.

What is wrong with this set of people who have paraded themselves as leaders in Nigeria? Why are the followers incapable of standing firm against these few souls who have held the country hostage, more vicious than kidnappers, bandits or terrorists?

Today the government has finally increased electricity tariff to honor the advice from IMF and World Bank eggheads, yet not very long ago, the same government to the knowledge of these agents in the above financial institutions, spent 16 billion dollars to improve the electricity delivery to Nigerian but we harvested more darkness. The era of men and women in key positions bringing foreign investors carried the scandal away.

Our criminal acts and inefficiency has brought more sorrow to the people: the electricity distribution companies neither repairs install or replace existing items that have collapsed donkeys of months ago. Even ordinary electric poles and cables are provided by consumers. Prepaid meters that were installed in uncompleted buildings in other countries like Ghana could not be provided in Nigeria unless the consumer, desperate to avoid Estimated Billing regime agrees to pay for meter and also pay the distribution company workers for the installation exercise. Now the inefficiency and human shortsightedness prevalent in the electricity subsector has pushed the government to hike tariff in order to appease the oracles called Distribution Companies as if tariff increment would bring solution to the crises in the system.

I feel very sad whenever I see the distribution company workers or agents going around with ladders just to intimidate consumers. They do not want to install prepaid meters because estimated billing will stop and illegal revenue will cease. They do not carry ladders around to carry out maintenance of failed system but to force consumers to part with their money, either paying the estimated bills or massaging the field workers' private pockets so their dreams of owning SUVs will be met and a thanksgiving will be done in the church.

The distribution companies are owned by the same leaders; the Regulatory body is the same leaders or their agents. The Generation and Transmission companies are the same people: the hands of Esau, the voice of Jacob. When and how shall the oppressed be free from oppression?

It is always painful to remember the sad past: how the sailors from Europe discovered the new world and needed men, women and children to work on the land for quicker production that led to the industrial explosion in Europe. And these workforces were carried forcefully with chains on their legs and necks to eliminate resistance. The African leaders who sold the slaves at the time were rewarded with rum, mirror and gun powder

Today the African leaders are encouraged to hide the proceeds of their financial ravages in the developed nations, encouraged also to surround themselves with SUVs, Airplanes, properties around the globe so that the 3rd world will remain the supplier of cheap manpower, this time without chains.

CHAPTER FOUR

The pathway to Restoration

Having analyzed the problems afflicting this nation which boils down to leadership greed and thirst for foreign products as Walter Rodney summarized in his book: "How Europe Underdeveloped Africa", the great question demands a way forward. Shall we remain stagnated at a point and pass blames on our shameless leadership, waiting to continue the blame culture on their offspring who are being nurtured by their parents to take over after their inglorious passage?

There is no problem on earth that has no solution. Human mistakes and frailties could become the weapons for growth. Ability to realize these mistakes of the past and endeavor not to continue in it signifies a departure from the past and a march into the future with enthusiasm as the atmosphere at independence in 1960 showed. The leeches of our hope for a better world represented by greedy leadership must give way. When people who are afflicted realizes the cause of their affliction and goes a step further to reject or denounce such things that bring the affliction, restoration physically and spiritually begins to come forth. But when the people do not know the cause of their problem, they will remain in the wilderness for too long. Divine intervention in the problems of the earth, whether natural or man-made does not come until nearly every one of the people feel the pinch. Israel remained in the land of Egypt until virtually every one, adult or children began to experience the hardship of their existence. It was then that they remembered the Promise Land. When a percentage of the populace still enjoys the benefit of leadership greed and avariciousness, the Creator does not intervene. Divine help comes quicker on individual basis than for a nation.

However when we see poor leadership manifestation as a window to greater opportunities and achievement in life, then we can surmount whatever looks like obstacle at the moment. Migrating to other nations is not the solution. As long as we see Nigeria as our collective inheritance, then we must stand shoulder to shoulder and shout at the devil and his agents afflicting us severely at present. We must be ready to lay down our lives for the sake of our children. Running away like dog with our tails behind is to give more room to the enemies of progress to continue the life of depravity. If Judas Iscariot did not collect money to betray the son of man, perhaps the ultimate sacrifice on the cross would be hard to come by. And what happens if Jesus Christ decided at the eleventh hour not to take the punishment of the world upon himself, shall we obtain that spiritual reconciliation with our Creator? The truth is that we must pay a price for the sake of freedom. Nigerians running away to other lands at the moment are merely postponing the evil day.

The children of Jacob thought it was wise to sell Joseph off and stop the continuous partiality of their father, Jacob. They believed that this partiality gave him the misplaced feeling in his dreams. No sibling allows favoritism from parents unless there is a true incapacitation of the favored child.

However the great famine that necessitated the journey into Egypt turned out to become a Divine plan of the Creator to preserve his chosen race and Joseph was the arrowhead of that sojourn into a foreign land. History is replete with stories of this nature which later became like the rejected stone.

China under Chairman Mao closed the borders for several years until the Chinese citizens imbibed a new spirit to conquer their environment. Today wherever the image of the Chinese man is seen, the controlling foreign power of such nation becomes restless. Adversity opens the door of success to a people in search of opportunities. Nigerians do not want to face any adversity, most especially the leaders whose reach to the spoils of office creates distraction to their spirits first, then the spirit of fear that if they refused to steal, tomorrow would be pitiable for them and their offspring takes over.

What manifest in the political group, affects the religious group too. They see drawbacks as failure, not a turning point for better approach to life issues. The graph of life journey is not a straight line but a line of ups and downs. There are seasons of joy and seasons of sadness, a time of growth and a time of fall. Mountains and Valleys are carved into human growth by the Creator. The Valley experiences are as necessary just as the Mountain experiences are needed.

The problems of African leaders lie in their expectations. They want to live like the foreigners without struggling to replicate the actions of these foreigners over the years which turned their environment better and better with each passing year. They are fully aware that these foreign lands with stable economy and political atmosphere did not just spring up overnight. When the challenges of governance overwhelm these African leaders as it must be, they relapsed into self-improvement. *"If I cannot change my environment, at least I can change my life and my offspring"* becomes like a mantra in their last effort at leadership. This is the roadmap that leads to looting, self-aggrandizement and all the shortcomings in leadership. But it is like cutting the nose to spite the Face! In a land of dilapidated road network, hunger and strife, only you and your family members are seen in glittering SUVs, private airplanes, suffocated in the abundance of life and you think you have won the race? The cries around will ultimately consume you and your family members. That was what the French revolution of 1914 brought to the surface. This becomes their primary fears, so they surround themselves with security details, even when they are out of power. But this will never guarantee the peace of mind needed to continue the journey of life!

Man can turn his adversities to windows of joy if he so desires. Indira Gandhi of India was killed by her security guards. Many leaders in history have died from the hands of their security covers. Africa and Nigeria are no exceptions. The coups in the history of this nation were perpetrated by the security arm of the government. Today the leaders may luxuriate in the knowledge that the security arm is in their payroll . But as long as they are not eager to guarantee effective leadership and put a stop to this continuous migration of our present and potential workforces, they are just like men sleeping with one eye closed.

In 1914, Nigeria was amalgamated by Lord Lugard for the economic wellbeing of his masters in United Kingdom. At the time in question, the Northern and Southern part of Nigeria have differing world views that seemed irreconcilable but today, the tide has changed; the floodgate of knowledge and modernity has come to eliminate much of the frictions in relationship. Nigerians have come to acknowledge that religion and ethnicity are no longer the drawbacks in their lives. All they need now is to stop the leaders who have been manipulating their lives for decades using religion and ethnicity as instruments of disagreement because when it comes to looting the commonwealth, the leaders are in perpetual harmony with each other; when it comes to kidnapping and massacre, the victims are not segregated on religious and ethnic divide. The people have come to understand that buying of properties abroad and establishing refineries outside the country are the masterminds of the leaders. The citizens now know that the habits of leaders from the South are the same with leaders from the North; all they are after is to enrich their private pockets at the expense of the majority.

Recently when a leader was confronted with possibility of the nation splitting into several countries, he laughed and said confidently:

"Nigerians are too poor to revolt" ... Nigeria cannot break up

because members of the elite are united in preserving their

advantages over the masses irrespective of the differences

of tribe and religion. "Nigeria," he said, "is too weak to break.

Who will break it? The ordinary person in Jigawa or the ordinary

person in Sokoto or the ordinary person in Bayelsa? Is it the Igbo

vulcanizer or the Yoruba woman selling kerosene by
the   roadside or the okada man in Delta? They don't have the
    capacity to unite because they are burdened by poverty.
            We have taken away from them their dignity, their self-esteem,
            their pride and self-worth so that they cannot even organize.
        "Up there, we (elite) unite….. we will never allow Nigeria
    to break because once it breaks, we will lose. But the common
        man loses nothing. What is he losing? He is already in hell;
        he cannot lose anything more than this hell"

This is the mindset of the leaders who are yearly jostling to rule Nigeria and bring the common man to the promise land!

Check the statistics: We spent 16 billion U.S Dollars on electricity but harvested darkness because the leaders and their cohorts were in private agreement to present contractors who disappeared with the contract money paid up front. The masses were never considered. It was the era when every Dick and Harry was in the forefront to bring in foreign investors in Nigeria. Even Local Government Chairmen's wives travelled to South Africa to scout for foreign investors!

As Foreign Essential Commodities (Essenco) impoverished Nigeria, so foreign investors did to Nigeria wealth! The modus operandi is like this: As a leader touched down at Murtala Mohammed International Airport in Lagos or Nnamdi Azikiwe International Airport in Abuja with plane A, the dubious foreign investor lands with plane B to sign off huge contracts and take the next flight out of the country immediately the money is paid into the company's account.

The masses have come to the conclusion that keeping silent or migrating out of the country does not constitute the solution to leadership recklessness. At present, many pockets of resistance are building up for the salvation of this nation. Once they are in place, alignment and re-alignment will come to blossom in the group and reduce unproductive members. Then it will become a force devoid of sentiment of religion and ethnicity. It will become a vanguard for the emancipation.

At this point, the remnant of the country will have no place to run to. When this is done, as experienced in Ghana, all that migrated: the workforce and the students, would return and the journey of a new Nigeria will begin.

It is the best option now. Apparently the expectation of the colonial masters is to see the nation divide in the near future. They merely stood firm for one indivisible country during the civil war because the leadership was still in their firm control. It takes a little spark of internal growth to change the tide. When leaders stop syphoning the commonwealth abroad, stop property purchase abroad and return every wealth back into the country, the economic gains behind the amalgamation of different nations into one will become a nightmare to the rest of the world. Nigeria will surpass China in human and capital development. And with Nigeria in the forefront of the struggle for true freedom, other African nations will look inwards: other countries of the earth will come to Africa when the continent is at the peak threshold of development.

Corruption is the antithesis of development. Imagine the stark reality before our very eyes! The crude oil is given to us by the Creator, not only to harvest but refine for other neighboring nations to buy. Unfortunately we allowed the greed of few people in positions of authority to change the roadmap. Today we import finished products of the same crude oil because these few souls in positions of leadership have established refineries outside Nigeria.

When you hear some leaders talk about product smuggling, you realize immediately that you are dealing with agents of the powers that be or simply the people who lacks the appropriate knowledge. Do business men and women smuggle Chinese products into their country? By looking inwards, the Chinese citizens produce many things and sell at a cheaper rate to the rest of the world, suffocating other countries' products that have high price tags. Most often, the consumers hardly look at the qualities of the products, but the ease of getting them at affordable prices. And sometimes, consumers hardly spare time to access its effectiveness.

If the nature and quantity of minerals in Nigeria is given to China as their birthright, it will be difficult for other nations around Nigeria to establish refineries in their country. The cost of buying finished products from Nigeria will be cheaper than establishing and managing a refinery in their country. All that is needed is a worthy sea going vessel to load finished products from our jetties. The favorable climate and fruitful landmass will bring the "Chinese products" to dominate the world market.

But our leaders do not have the mindset of the Chinese. Surrounded by ministers, commissioners, special assistants that knew next to nothing except propaganda, our leaders enter willingly into suspended animation. Imagine the utterances of a Special Assistant to a government: He opined that if Dangote refinery begin to refine crude oil and sell, we should not expect the products to be sold at the former rate (PMS 195 naira) of pump price of the product in the country because the investor spent several billions of dollars to establish the refinery. Unless the society does not want the investor to recoup his investment!

These and other statements from a battalion of ignorant humans that walk the Nigeria space as Special Assistants to leaders! How then can an ignorant leader who manipulated his way into power provide the dividends of democracy to the followers?

Nelson Mandela, the former president of South Africa and the hero of apartheid struggle in South Africa, said to Nigerians 2007:

"You know I am not very happy with Nigeria. I have made
   that very clear on many occasions. Yes, Nigeria stood by
   us more than any nation, but you let yourself down, and
   Africa and the black race very badly. Your leaders have no
   respect for their people. They believe that their personal
   interests are the interests of the people. They take
   people's resources and turn it into personal wealth.
   There is a level of poverty in Nigeria that should
   be unacceptable. I cannot understand why
   Nigerians are not more angry than they are.
"What do young
   Nigerians think about your leaders and their country and Africa?
   Do you teach them history…?
   "What about the corruption and the crimes? Your elections
   are like wars. Now we hear that you cannot be president in
   Nigeria unless you are Muslim or Christian. Some people tell me
   your country may break up. Please don't let it happen.
   '

"Let me tell you what I think you need to do. You
    should encourage leaders to emerge who will
not confuse public
    office with sources of making personal wealth.
Corrupt people
    do not make good leaders. Then you have to
spend a lot of your
    resources for education. "Educate children of
the poor,
    so that they can bring changes.   Poor,
uneducated
    people can also bring change, but it will be
hijacked by
    the educated and the wealthy…..give young
Nigerians
    good education. Teach them the value of hard
    work and sacrifice, and discourage them from
crimes
    which are destroying your image as a people"

REFERENCES

Walter Rodney: How Europe Underdeveloped Africa (1972)

Ndubuisi Obi Theophilus: NIGERIA: The Years of the Locust (2008)

Ndubuisi Obi Theophilus: The Evils that Men Do(2008)

Ndubuisi Obi Theophilus: The Hand of Esau, The Hand of Jacob(2009)

Ndubuisi Obi Theophilus: Behind the Mask(2009)

The Holy Bible, NIV.

www.ingramcontent.com/pod-product-compliance
Lightning Source LLC
Chambersburg PA
CBHW051832250726
48659CB00005B/1798